new songs

poems by
otto h. selles

relief prints by
geraldine selles-ysselstein

published by
pandora press
kitchener, ontario
2001

National Library of Canada Cataloguing in Publication Data

Selles, Otto H.
New songs: poems

Includes bibliographical references.
ISBN 1-894710-14-2

1. Christian poetry, Canadian (English) I. Selles-Ysselstein, Geraldine II. Title.

PS3619.E44N48 2001   811'.6   C2001-902861-X

Some of the poems and prints have been published previously. Our thanks to the editors of the following journals and magazines for giving us permission to reprint these works:

"my square inch," *The Banner*, January 4, 1999, p. 38 (poem).
"tulip," *Perspectives. A Journal of Reformed Thought*, November 2000, p. 17 (poem and print).
"like what," *Perspectives. A Journal of Reformed Thought*, November 2000 (print, cover art).
"growing," *The Banner*, January 1, 2001, p. 27 (poem and print).
"death drops," *Books and Culture. A Christian Review*, January/February 2001, p. 42 (poem and print).

The quotation on page 86 is taken from James D. Bratt, ed., *Abraham Kuyper: A Centennial Reader* (Grand Rapids, MI: W. B. Eerdmans, 1998), p. 488.
The meditation quoted on page 87 is taken from Lionel Basney, "Meditations for Lent: Third Sunday, 'The Turn,'" in *The Banner* (February 1999) and is used with permission.

This book was published with the aid of the Calvin Center for Christian Scholarship, Calvin College, Grand Rapids, Michigan.

NEW SONGS

Copyright © 2001 by Pandora Press
33 Kent Avenue Kitchener, Ontario, N2G 3R2

Co-published with Herald Press
Scottdale, Pennsylvania/Waterloo, Ontario

International Standard Book Number 1-894710-14-2
Printed in Canada on acid-free paper

09 08 07 06 05 04 03 02 01   10 9 8 7 6 5 4 3 2 1

to the memory of our parents
Gerry Akkerman-Selles (1921-1988)
Lubbertus Selles (1915-1993)

contents

preface

I once read an essay that suggested the study of poetry as
the best preparation for a degree in law. Forget about political
science or economics as the base of a legal education, said
the author, and study Donne or Dickinson instead. After
all, every attorney must learn to read texts closely, including
those that are dense with ambiguity. Let poets take him to
school.

Perhaps poetry-reading as job-training is better than no
reading at all, but aren't there better reasons for getting into a
poem? In a famous essay, Matthew Arnold said that a poem's
great power is "to awaken in us a wonderfully full, new, and
intimate sense of things, and of our relations with them." A
poet helps us not only to see and hear the old world afresh,
but also to enter a new world and dwell there for a time. Poets
"dream dreams and see visions." They imagine possible worlds
and invite readers into them.

By accepting the invitation, a reader finds herself deepened
and expanded. We are sometimes timid souls, content with
routine observations and with clichés to express them. Worse,
the older we get, the smaller our world. But poets are like
prophets. They have been sent by God to challenge business
as usual. When we absorb a good poem (John Ciardi wrote
that we inhale it), something happens that is more easily
experienced than described. Our sympathies widen, our
imagination quickens, our longing awakens like a child on the
first day of summer. In other words, the Spirit of God begins
to blow and we hear new songs.

Somebody has to write the songs; hence my gratitude for
this wonderful new collection of poems by Otto Selles. In a
variety of moods and humors from droll to almost terrifying,
Selles explores biblical and spiritual themes with great
ingenuity. Here's a case where the poet is interested in the
themes, not just in his reaction to the themes. Much
contemporary poetry is embarrassingly self-referential: the
author explores the layers of his own disorientation, convinced
that others will find the tour as fascinating as he does. But

Selles shines a light outward, and from various angles, so that we may see anew what has always been there, or see for the first time possibilities beyond our usual ken.

In part I, "cymbals," the author takes up familiar words or phrases and bends them so that we may find in them more facets of meaning. Metaphors such as "slice of life" or acronyms like "tulip" expand to reincorporate some of the literal features of bread and flowers. Familiar objects —"stone," "palm"— gather to themselves a wealth of biblical reference. An ambiguous phrase, "death drops," turns one way and then another, till we have seen life and death from a place we had not been before.

Part II, "lyres," gives us mostly dramatic monologues in which the author takes an extraordinary point of view. We see a biblical, or simply human, landscape through the eyes of Goliath, or the elder brother, or Judas. The man from Jesus' parable who buried his one talent gets to defend himself, and does so with remarkable pathos. Always the poems bring us little grenades of surprise that go off as we read them: heaven, for example, is actually illumined by way of teenage mall-speak ("like what").

In part III, "strings," we find poems with a wider range of feelings and points of view, including pieces whose narrator is a child, or a person with an obsession, or even a handful of seed. Sometimes the juxtaposition of a lyrical and a distressing theme ("shepherd") gives the reader a jolt similar to the sort one feels in reading the metaphysical poems of, say, Richard Crashaw.

This collection — so inventive, so alive with intelligence — is wonderfully complemented by the art of Geraldine Selles-Ysselstein. The result is striking. Altogether, what we get is what Matthew Arnold promised, and in a way he hadn't intended. Arnold looked at the Sea of Faith and heard "only its melancholy, long, withdrawing roar." At such a time especially, we sense how much we need awakened in us "a wonderfully full, new, and intimate sense of things, and of our relations with them."

For that we'll need some new songs.

Cornelius Plantinga Jr.
President-Elect of Calvin Theological Seminary

new songs

I will sing
to you
new songs
played upon
clashing cymbals
voiced with
pure lyres
danced upon
taut strings

part I

cymbals

my square inch

one square inch
inch by inch
line by line
I drew it out
side by side
face by face
and said, "that's mine"

above the inch
the square inch
I wrung my hands
inch by inch
then clipped
my heart to a line
and drip by drip
by drip
inched into the square
my square inch

my brain
(sides both right and left)
did not complain as I
boiled it
scooping off the foam
into my inch

and as I hold my
square inch up to the light
I must believe
it belongs to me
and not to you

tulip

there is something
depraved about a tulip
staying totally hidden
all summer fall and winter
in the dirt

there is something
smug about a tulip
electing as it does to bloom
when spring conditions are perfect

there is something
miserly about a tulip
as it attempts to atone for its long absence
with such a limited appearance

but it's very hard
to hold a grudge against a tulip
as it moves irresistibly
through rock hard ground
and clumps of crusty snow
to shoot up green and gracious
to meet the spring sun
and burst into open color

still there is something
a bit defeatist about a tulip
unable to persevere against wind and rain
unable to stop silken petals from falling
as stem and leaves droop
and die yellow and brown
leaving an unsaintly mess
in an untilled garden

slice of life

often you are too hard
for me to swallow
you stick in my throat
dry crusty crumbling
totally stale

or you are completely bland
enriched soggy white
with nothing to chew on
I try to swallow but you stick
in my throat with nothing
nothing to wash you down

stone

am I
a stumbling
stone blocking
your way
be the first
to roll
such a stone
away

am I
a stepping
stone standing
only now
and then
in your way
be the first
to cast
such a stone
away

am I
an unturned
stone deaf to
your way
be the first
to corner
such a stone
and fashion it
to hear
your way

family

perhaps our family is most like a tree
with strong roots searching deep into the dark soil
to gather water to add another circle
to an ever widening trunk
that stands solid below branches heavy and long
stretching out to protect the ground
or rising to grasp the sky
with slender twigs and tender leaves
each leaf different in size and shade
yet shaped in the same form
and each leaf joined to a twig
to a branch to the trunk to the roots
that hold the tree as it sways in the wind
as leaves shine dark then light
as branches touch each other
and clap and whistle with the leaves

but our family is too often like a tree
with a hollow trunk and dry roots
and far too many broken branches
with too much dead wood
too many fallen leaves

maybe it is best to hope
our family is most like a rope
and the best image we can afford
is woven with every sort of cord
some short some long
some worn some strong
some white some red
all bound of one accord
into a single thread
sewn through a single word

before our family gets caught up in some rope
you say you prefer our family as a tree
but may I note that both
trees and cords can share knots
so our family can be a tree
if you allow me to attach a cord
and swing back and forth
and whistle with the leaves

if you stand at a cross
roads and wonder
which way to turn
move cross
wise to meet me

if you carry a cross
chained to your neck
throw yourself
into the sea
and you will float a
cross to me

if you lift high a cross
bones flying below a skull
drop those bones
and cross through
that skull to me

if you reach a cross
to take my hand
give your fingers
and your heart
and cross them
with me

palm

you hold me in the palm
of your hand
and I nestle
in a crease

you hold me in the palm
of your hand
raised to bless
and I fall
into the air

you catch me in the palm
of your hands
joined to pray
and I drink
sweat and blood

I hold your palm
open as a leaf
and I wave
that palm
as a branch

I hold that palm open
and I strike
with my palm
as a hammer
on a nail

and you seize me with the palm
of your hand
as a nail holds
and will
not let go

death drops

a needle rain
falls
each time
death
drops
in

rust
and regret
fill
each eye
each time
death
drops
by

but you drank
one time
all death
drops
and you wipe
each eye
to pour out
life springs

part II

lyres

garden

now tell me
did you have
to stretch to grab to pull
or did it just seem to fall
ripe with promises into your
open hands

did you have to use your fingers
to press to pierce to divide
it quickly into sections
before greedily thrusting
piece after piece into your
eager mouth

or was it soft and wet with dew
as you brought it slowly to your face
to feel to sense to smell
before your teeth tenderly
broke the skin
and you touched it lightly with your
fleshy tongue

when you had eaten
did you seek him out
to offer to give to pass
a section
a half-eaten portion from your
dripping fingers

and did you have
to explain to coax to plead
or did he quickly take it
to bite to chew to swallow
as you licked your
moist lips

did you
once he had finished
did you look at each other
with new eyes
filled with a different desire
only to look away
to look to the ground

to find some leaves
and did you then taste
something bittersweet
your hands and fingers sticky
your mouth closed
your tongue held between
trembling lips

giant

another day another curse
I'll get up if I must and face my face to
those cowards

give me now my helmet
help me sling the javelin across my back
and this sword I'd rather do without
it all weighs a ton

go ahead
let's move quickly to the lines
and be done with it
you know this is all getting to be such a bore

do you notice how they tremble just because I'm a bit tall
watch them shake even more
when they hear my spiel
as if they haven't heard it before
as if they are ever going to send anyone to fight me
I should just stay in bed tomorrow

say what's that kid doing there by the stream
tell him to play somewhere else
or I will sling him back to his folks
but stop
save the trip
he's coming our way

so what do we have here
a boy
a pretty boy as red as blood
did you stay out in the sun too long
go back to those comfy tents across the stream
it must be your nap time

well well you've come to challenge me have you now
look up
yes way up
and tell me

do you boy pretty boy
think I'm some little doggy that you can come here
and whack me with a stick

unfortunately my friend and I ate already
but you know those birds above your head
wouldn't mind a tasty morsel
and all the animals that roam about those fields
wouldn't mind a bite
so before I show you my culinary skills
take my advice and run along
that would be
a good thing

sure sure some big guy
in the sky is going to help you push me over
and with a chopper you'll chop off my head
then all my friends will be sliced and diced
and fed to the birds and beasts
sounds all very
philistine to me

look let me show you something
come here and check out
this sword
it's actually quite soft
so soft I can even pat it
now you
pat the sword

what do you got in your bag
come on let me see
playing games are we
here I'll put down my sword
and let me take off my helmet
just throw the rock right in here
come on
come on pitch it straight in here
you can do it
kid

yes let the stone fly
I see it coming
right

house

just pass me
that pillar of salt over there
it's a bit shorter than I
but will do well
for my own house
here on the sand

I did not ask you for your opinion
and even if you say it stands
a bit twisted
this pillar should hold
wouldn't you say
a window to look at
what was
before you pulled me along

be of some use and help me
attach this roof
so I can have some privacy for once
and if you will not lend a hand
notice this
finishing touch
a door
hanging
closed

one last thing
if you are still there
you would really
help me a lot
if you would just
leave me
alone
with this pillar
truly worthy of its salt
for I am beginning to savor its
quiet support
here on the sand

now don't start that knocking
you will break down the door
crack the window
cave the roof
topple the pillar
destroy my house

and do stop those tears
you will just
wash my house away
wash me
away
with the sand
with the pillar of salt

talent

now just a minute
let me say something
in my defense
I was careful
cautious
and prudent
to a fault
in your opinion

but remember
my respect for you
and your gift
for why should I have trusted
a bank in danger of being robbed
or some investment always on the edge
of crashing
of dissolving your capital
which I return
undiminished

and why compare me to that fellow
to him much has been given
and you are right
to demand an equal return
but I received little
and that little I return unbroken
for I acted in your interest
as a good and fearful servant

perhaps it has indeed
dulled a bit
from having sat so long
in the ground
here let me give it another polish
just let me
try again

all right
you will not listen
so I will go outside
I know how to grit my teeth
and you won't see me cry
but just let me say
you have hurt my feelings
very deeply

and another thing
it's unfair
so unfair
that I only received
one talent
and now
you take it
from
me

quickly

I thought
I had had enough of him
I thought
he had it coming to him
I had what I wanted
and he would get
what he deserved

I thought
I had to
from the way he looked at me
from the way he told me
to do
what I had to do
and to do it
quickly

but I never
really thought
he would come to any
real harm
that it would come
to this

take these pieces back
use them
to free him
to bring him
to take him
back

take
these pieces
I do not want
them
I do not care
for them

take them
take what I took
so eagerly
take back what
you gave
so readily

take these pieces then
with your feet
if your hands
cannot hold them
do with them
whatever you would like to do
and I will do
what I have left to do
and I will do it
quickly

brother

now wasn't that quite
a party
look at the shape of that
fattened calf
only bones and some skin now
just like you
hey come on
I'm just kidding
it's good we can talk
now the old man
has gone to bed

of course I'm happy
to see you
after all these years
I spent
slaving away in the fields
while
you spent
half of our fields

of course I'm happy
to see you
reconciled with the
old man
to see you
in these new clothes
alive when we all thought
you were dead
so of course
I'm happy
we celebrated
what was lost
has been found
we danced

we sang we ate
we were happy
so happy

but remember one thing
I am sick
and tired
of the shadows
of standing
in the background
looking over
the old man's shoulder
as he looked and
looked for you
and now you are back
now he only
has eyes for you
so just remember
all that
he has
is now mine
for all that
you had
you spent

of course I'm happy
to forgive you
but I will
never forget
you are now
my hired hand
and you will
never forget
that I'm happy
to be
my brother's keeper

disappearing act

where have you been
locked up somewhere
living in a cave or something
are you the only person who doesn't know
what happened

but say haven't we met somewhere before
you look familiar
fine fine don't get angry
as you say
we have never seen each other before

listen
I will tell you then what he was like
well he was what we thought he should be
you know turning tables
promising to destroy and raze everything
he also knew how to throw in some healing techniques
good stuff all
got the people on our side
and then he got caught and didn't have
much of a chance after that
believe me we were both ready to fight it out
but he wanted none of it
I don't know
sometimes he was
a hard act to follow

now my friend and me
get this
we just found out that some women we know
went to see the body and found nothing but
get this
some angels
yes angels telling them he's alive
so some of our guys go down and find

no body
and nobody
not one of those angels
it's just one big mystery to us now

look
don't call me a fool
I know all those promises as well as anyone
but I can see
I can see what you are getting at
we all have to suffer a bit
before we get what we want

now don't get all offended again
and act as if you've got somewhere to go
it's dark and you won't get anywhere
come stay with us here for the night
and share a bite to eat

it may be small but it's cheaper than in the city
I'm getting tired of the walk mind you
make yourself comfortable
while we try and find something to eat

here's some bread
go ahead take eat
but remember not all of it
break off a piece for me
I certainly need some
after all this walking and talking

when I see you there beside the lamp
I'm positive I've seen you before
why you know you certainly look
you look just like him

don't go don't be offended
come back
you can't just
disappear on us

like what

so what's heaven gonna be
like clouds and wings
like in a sunday comic
a bearded saint at the entry
with his book
checking it once
twice, you naughty, but you nice
either go back (to zero) or just
straight through
those pearly gates

so what's heaven gonna be
like halos and harps
like in a hymn
all around
the crystal sea
the streets paved with gold
walls built of gems
nothing to fix or make
nothing much to do
but sing

so what's heaven gonna be
like "hey, look who's here"
like in a class reunion
"is it really you
you haven't changed a bit
(surprised you could make it)"

so what's heaven gonna be
like totally different
like in an absolutely awesome movie
people transformed
in an instant
neither wrinkled nor bald
neither sick nor slow

just perfect
perfectly wiped clean
of all that was

so what's heaven gonna be
like another garden
like in the beginning
beautiful
but free
to touch every tree
is that
what heaven's gonna be

part III

strings

poe/try

a line
the shortest line
between two points
the crow flew
graceful
across the sky

but the crow stopped
weary and dreary
on a thin line
and croaked
and crowed
the same cry
as it jumped
from one line
to another thin line

suddenly the crow
found its prey and
plunged to the ground
and crow's feet
circled an eye
cautiously
before a beak
rapped tapped
and drew out
jagged lines of flesh

replete the crow
found its rest
in strings and yarns
and every kind of line
taken to feather its nest

frosty

you find my feet in bitter ice
and warn that I will perish twice
while my coldness provokes your hate
you tell me that your love is great
from what I've learned of your desire
I'd favor now a tongue of fire
for it would certainly suffice
to melt away these feet of ice

growing

you took me
and scattered me along
the open path over there
and I sat
and sat calmly
quietly
until some birds came
hopped close and began
nicely at first
to peck but then
they picked me apart

you then threw me
upon the rocks
and I somehow
put down some roots
but as I warmed up to things
my hard-nosed company
in the end
heated up as well
and I was the one
who got burned

you then cast me
the next time
among some thorns
and I learned to be careful
to bend and shift my way
but they in their piercing fashion
choked all my efforts
and I stood again
empty-handed

you finally threw me
onto a place where I found
no rocks no thorns and thankfully
no birds
and here I am
and here I sit
and wait
to start
growing

child

I am a child
with my childish ways
when you ask
for bread
I give you five stones
for fish
I offer two snakes

so all agree
that with these childish ways
I must be kept away
but you say
come
for I belong to you
despite my childish ways

sometimes

sometimes I too
can walk on water
water clear
and hard
reflecting my steps
as I move
to meet you

yet I stop on the water
to look down at my feet
as waves and wind
push me down
so you reach down
to take my hands
to save me
and chide me
for only walking on water
sometimes

pet dream

I took you in
small
nurtured you
first just with scraps and
wish bones
and then I gorged you
on feasts served
upon elaborate reflections
as I walked you
throughout my dull days

I taught you tricks
to roll over and over
in my mind
to sit up and beg
for more details
to play dead and suddenly
in a snap
to come to life
and fetch my thoughts

I felt I kept you well at heel
but you
unleashed in me
what had never crossed my mind
for your noisy bark bit
and broke my peace

yet each morning I place
your collar
around my neck
and you
keep me company
growing larger and larger
so that you even walk
through my eyes
closed to sleep

so it's high time to abandon you
to put you down
my too faithful
pet dream

valley

dry bones
upon the floor
of a valley
of bones
I was tossed

the bones
upon the valley floor
began to rattle
against
my bones
as tendons shot
from the ground
to join bone
to bone while
flesh and
skin rained
down covering
the bones
fixed still
to the valley floor

the four winds walked
into the valley
to breathe
breath into
the fleshy bones
that soon stood
as a vast army

and I also stood
and I too began
to march
out of the valley
as one body
among the
breathing bones

shepherd

if you are a shepherd
then I can be a lamb
dressed in my best
with the rest of the flock
I can sit and stand
huffing and puffing
songs and phrases
with enough vigor
to blow your house down

if you are a shepherd
then I can be a lamb
for wherever you will go
I am sure to follow
carrying bags of promises
one to fleece my master
one to appease my dame
and one to hush the little boy
who starves down the lane

but if you are a shepherd
then you can see me as I am
how big my eyes are
how big my teeth are
for the truth is
you pull the wool from my eyes
so I can see me as I am
the better you say to invite me
to a table you have prepared before me
for all is ready
to come
eat and drink
the lamb

thin volume

that book's cover
is indeed a bit worn
and the binding is beginning
to fray at the edges
inside
you will see
I am
half finished
half begun

go ahead
read what is written
in my ink
set in my type
grouped under my headings
punctuated with my thoughts

I realize the style is
at first tight and stiff
then loose and uneven
some cutting and pasting
some adding of footnotes
some deleting of certain passages
and certain chapters
may take out some of the
inconsistency

after a glance
you return the book
chuckle and slap me on the back
to say you can always read
between my lines
and you add that
I need to trust
in a well-wrought conclusion
to obtain depth
in a thin volume

This list offers the chief biblical, theological, and literary
texts upon which the poems are based.

new songs Psalms 96 and 150.

my square inch Refers to a phrase taken from a speech by the
Dutch theologian and statesman Abraham Kuyper (1837-
1920): "no single piece of our mental world is to be
hermetically sealed off from the rest, and there is not a square
inch in the whole domain of our human existence over which
Christ, who is Sovereign over *all*, does not cry: 'Mine!'"

tulip Acronym often used in Reformed theology to explain the
doctrine of predestination (total depravity, unconditional election,
limited atonement, irresistible grace, preservation or perseverance
of the saints).

slice of life For communion: Luke 22: 19-20;
I Corinthians 11: 28.

stone Luke 24: 1-3; John 8: 7; Acts 4: 11-12; Ephesians
2: 19-20.

family Rahab the prostitute: Joshua 2: 15-18 and 6: 25;
Matthew 1: 5-6; Hebrews 11: 31.

cross Jeremiah 6: 16; Matthew 10: 38; 18: 6; and 27: 33;
hymn text by George W. Kitchin, "Lift High the Cross";
Matthew 11: 28-29.

palm For Palm Sunday: Psalm 139: 9-10; Mark 10: 16;
Luke 22: 44; John 12: 13; Revelation 7: 9; Matthew 27:
30; John 19: 18.

death drops Revelation 7: 17 and 21: 4; John 7: 37-38.

garden Eve: Genesis 3: 1-8.

giant David and Goliath: I Samuel 17.

house Lot's wife: Genesis 19: 26; Revelation 3: 20;
Luke 6: 46-49.

talent Parable of the talents: Matthew 25: 14-30.

quickly Judas at the temple: John 13: 27; Matthew 27: 3-5.

brother The prodigal son's elder brother: Luke 15: 11-32.

disappearing act The disciples on the road to Emmaus: Luke 24: 13-35.

like what Revelation 4-5; hymn text by William Kuipers, "By the Sea of Crystal"; Revelation 21-22: 1-5; I Thessalonians 4: 13-18; I Corinthians 15: 52-53, Genesis 2: 15-17.

poe/try Edgar Allan Poe, "The Raven."

frosty For Pentecost: Robert Frost, "Fire and Ice"; Matthew 24: 12; Revelation 3: 15; Acts 2: 3.

growing Parable of the sower: Matthew 13: 3-9.

child Jesus and children: John 6: 9; Luke 11: 11; Matthew 19: 13-15.

sometimes Peter walking on water: Matthew 14: 28-31.

pet dream For Lent: "What do we repent of? In the Bible it is often idolatry — putting the wrong thing at the center of our lives. Or it is an outright wrong, done on impulse or by design. It is the favorite anger, the nurtured grudge, the stab of envy, the pet dream of greed or lust or power. It is our preoccupation with ourselves." Lionel Basney in *The Banner*, February 1999.

valley Ezekiel 37: 1-14.

shepherd For Good Shepherd Sunday: John 10: 11; Psalm 23; Matthew 26: 26-28; John 1: 29; Revelation 5: 12.

acknowledgments

Numerous people have provided inspiration, help, and encouragement in preparing this collection. I would like to thank in particular Glenn Fetzer, Henrietta Ten Harmsel, Barbara Carvill, Darlene Meyering, Cindy de Jong, Mike Van Denend, Jim Bratt, Donna Romanowski, and, especially, pastors Duane Kelderman and Carl Kammeraad of Neland Ave. Christian Reformed Church (Grand Rapids, Michigan). Max Eerdmans, Bob Hudson, and Bob de Moor were extremely generous with their time and assistance. Jim Vanden Bosch, Hugh Cook, Francis Fike, David Timmer, Bob VanderMolen, Deb and Hank Meijer, Luci Shaw, and the late Lionel Basney provided useful comments and suggestions. I am thankful to my wife, Rita, for lending her critical eye to the examination of each poem's multiple drafts, and to my children, Anna, Isabelle, and Luc, for sharing in the pleasure of reading nursery rhymes, Edward Lear, and Dr. Seuss.

Geraldine wishes to thank Jean Little for her encouragement, Margaret Priest for her insights as an instructor, Chris S. Overvoorde and Helen Bonzelaar for their leadership in the visual arts, her husband Peter and three daughters, Geraldine Jr., Margaretha, and Johanna for their support and insights into the artist's life and to Otto, whose "new songs" have brought about this collaboration.

We are very grateful to our editor, C. Arnold Snyder, for guiding the book to press and to Nathan Stark for his design work. Our thanks to Neal Plantinga for his support of this project from its outset. We acknowledge the generous aid provided by the Calvin Center for Christian Scholarship. Finally, both Geraldine and I would like to thank our sister Johanna for cheering us up and along the way through her daily affirmations.

Otto H. Selles, *Grand Rapids, Michigan*
Geraldine R. Selles-Ysselstein, *Arkell, Ontario*

DATE DUE

Demco, Inc 38-293